Crushes on Buses
A Collection of Stories

I0162512

Diane K Gough

FOR DANIEL BROWN

Thank you for a pure heart, inside of you lies a school bus everyone wants to ride. You are as magical as magic can possibly get.

CONTENTS

I HOPE WE END UP LOVING, MY LOVE

I hope this infatuation will end up being love, my love.
I hope when you look at me, you see more than just a
pretty girl, love. I hope I'm more than just some girl you
think you could save; although, I know you are brave
enough to.

But once you save me, once you've knocked down my
wall and it comes tumbling down, will you still chase?
Will you still find me whimsical, all new wave? Or will
you run to the next girl?

I see the way you look at me; I don't think it's love.
But I still like the way you look at me.
Those eyes will burn for a new girl, and I know that too,
but I still want us to be two. We'd be so cute and calm,
like my favorite color blue.

You are driving me all sorts of crazy, and I kind of feel
lazy, cause all I ever do is sit back and think of you. Oh
please don't make me blue and say you'll love me too. I
remember when I wore my favorite dress, your jaw
dropped and my heart stopped. Oh, I hope we end up
loving, my love.

I like how our handshake turned into high fives, and our
high fives turned into hand holdings, and our hand
holdings turned into hugs. Oh why don't you kiss me!
Let's make this steady already!

I've never liked cuddling, but it sounds good with you. A lot of things I haven't done before sound good with you. There's a lot of things I haven't done that I'd want to do with you my love,
like love.

WHEN YOUR HIGH SCHOOL CRUSH PASSES AWAY

When you find out, you remember the way your history teacher used to call his name. He always dragged it "Sunnnyy," which causes you to smile because your history teacher was your favorite teacher. Since Sunny was known to be a trouble-maker, the way he smiled and talked to Mr. Mueller makes you believe that maybe that was his favorite teacher also.

You can't believe it's been three years. It feels like it was just yesterday that Mr. Mueller reassigned seats and you sat behind Sunny. He asked for a pencil, and you gave him your best one, hoping he'd give it back, but it would be okay if he didn't. It's difficult to remember if he did or didn't, perhaps it has been three years. You hope he didn't since it would be the only gift you'd give him in this life.

It's hard to process this; I mean he was Sunny. Sunny was always cool. You pictured him introducing you to rock songs you hadn't heard of yet. He had a lip piercing and all; he was Sunny. He spoke to teachers the way he wanted to. He was the definition of "too cool for school" and too cool for you.

His eyes were always droopy, and you didn't know why. They often looked sad. You wondered if his girlfriend knew that maybe her boyfriend was somber. As you saw them making out in the hallway, you wondered if physical intimacy was all they ever had. You wanted to think that if only he knew you, maybe he wouldn't be so sad. There's love songs you could have introduced him to.

He wasn't like the other boys you always wanted, so you never told your friends. You can't even remember if you and him had the same lunch hour. No matter how close you were to him, he always seemed other worldly. Like no matter the miles you ran, you would never actually get to him.

Last week you were driving near your old high school, and although you are quite classy about these things, you stuck out your middle finger. It was nothing other than an acknowledgment of knowing you would never have to return. Today, you logged on Facebook and mutual friends led you to see the "REST IN PEACE" phrase plastered near the beloved Sunny's tagged photos. Cool Sunny, Sunny with the lip piercing, Sunny with the good music.

Graduation day was the first time you saw light in his eyes. Happy Sunny. Your last name started with a B and his with a G. You looked a few heads behind and there he was, ready to get out and live his life. Standing almost like he was too cool to care that he was graduating, but not too cool to smile.

You saw him a few months after graduation day. He didn't have a lip piercing anymore. His hair was different now, less bold, no streaks of red or green. He was holding hands with a new girl, not the girl he used to kiss in the hallway. This girl seemed loving, the type of girl that would embrace him first before planting a kiss on his lips. You were sitting at a fast-food place with a friend, and you almost said hi, but he wouldn't have recognized you. After all, you can't recognize someone you don't know. I don't think he knew that you sat behind him or that you gave him your best pencil. It's possible that he didn't even know your name, but his name was Sunny; Sunny with the good music and the lip piercing.

I Am Your Biggest Fan

I had a flash flood warning message delivered to my phone this morning. Even the earth agrees that I've been thinking of you too much, I'm flooding my space. I'm sinking on purpose to see if you happen to be at the bottom of the ocean. If you do happen to be there lying dead and still, I plan on joining you. I imagine by the time I reach the bottom of the ocean all the energy I have will be gone, but if you happen to be alive, I'll swim back to the top of the ocean for the both of us.

I don't ever want to make your life harder than it already is. I want to be the everlasting rainbow outside of your backyard. I want to tell you that I love you, not just in words but I want my smile to be the eternal proof of my "I love you's." I want to write a song for you. When I sing these songs for you, I hope you no longer find birds and bugs fascinating, but my love if you do, I'll sing you a song for that too.

I will caress the roughest parts of you, and if it leaves these gentle hands of mine bleeding, I'll use my feet. I will let you have as many anxiety attacks as you please. I will never be ashamed of them or of you.

I will make you the hero of all the scars you own on your body. I'll clap first, and I'll clap last. I will exaggerate these stories because I am your biggest fan. I will never eat fruits like Grapefruit and Olives, I want my lips to be forever sweet to you when you kiss them. So I'll stick to Mango's and Peaches, but I won't eat apples. I don't want to expel you from this garden of Eden if it's the greatest peace you've ever encountered.

I've raised you from the ocean, tilted my head, given you two full breathes and compression until you've recovered. I am your biggest fan.

Me And All Of The People That Loved You

We caught every tantrum you threw with our bare hands and let it skin our palms, without shedding a tear. You became the king who hadn't fought for his crown, but it was given to you with honor. We stayed up past twelve for you and buried ourselves in dry soil for you. We suffocated for you. With all your nothings, we still proclaimed you King.

We feared you but danced with you to all the songs you played. Especially me, I swayed. My feet galloped to the dance floor for you. We gave it our all. I wrote poems I'm sure could have ended a war, but you laughed and said they would begin them. When I wasn't in the same room as you, I felt like I could touch the sky and fall asleep on the moon.

We wrapped you in the warmest blanket while we shivered at the future you placed before us. You never apologized, you were just full of apologies, and I wish my forgiving heart knew the difference. There were days where I became your biggest fan. You would make me laugh so hard that my nose would bleed and my guts would explode. Maybe that was just a way of killing me slowly. But in those days, I was so sure that everything would be okay.

I tried to convince everyone that had loved you, that you were worth loving, and that you were worth being crowned both King and Queen. I wrote poems that woke flowers in those days, and those flowers woke me up, and I never wanted to die. I played songs foreign to my guitar with the sweetest sounds and melodies that woke God's angels up. I loved every minute of being alive. I couldn't believe I ever wanted to not be so. I wrote poems that could have ended wars, and you believed in them. You believed in me, in me and all the people that loved you. We believed in you, we believed in each other.

You never apologized, but your eyes had. And my forgiving heart had to be okay with it. You galloped to the dance floor for us. You danced to our songs, especially to mine, you swayed. I felt like I could touch the sky and fall asleep on the moon. I've learned not to listen to every word you pronounce. I've learned to let go. I don't want to crash my car anymore; no need to die when you can dance. Maybe we loved you so much, and you didn't know how to catch all that love with your bare hands without skinning your palms. You shed a tear that ended up drowning me and all the people that loved you. And still, we love you.

How To Not Fall In Love With Her Boy

I come home. I tell myself, "take your heart, yank it off, and throw it on the floor. Step on it so hard until you can no longer read the name of that boy. When she talks to you about him, remember to smile and have good posture. Give that old friend a chance, the one who's been begging for a date." I take a deep breath and tell myself, "Your feelings, they are rotten. Have no feelings. You got this."

I should have known that I wouldn't give myself a pep talk if I "got" this. Developing feelings for a person is scary, annoying and exciting, especially when you know you shouldn't like them.

I hate when it slowly creeps up on you. For example, you and this person have always liked the same band, but all of a sudden you guys "like" the same band, and you begin to think it's a sign. You begin to wonder why your friend even shows interest for this person. You know this person so much more. It's like asking God for the right person to show up, but when the right person shows up, you're not there to open the door. Instead, your friend opens the door and says hi to your right person.

Maybe you were in the bathroom while they struck up a conversation. Maybe you were working when they decided to hangout. Maybe they both had the same class. Whatever it was, your friend and this person became close, and she developed feelings for him.

However, you and this person begin to know each other way more. Late-night conversations along with night walks that make you feel both guilty and beautiful. You plan a hangout for this person and your friend in hopes that they can get to know each other better. In hopes that maybe your rotten feelings will go away.

Your friend is oblivious, she's just happy that she's in the same room as her crush. And you're oblivious too at first. You're not acting like yourself. This person excites you. You make them laugh, and they make you smile, but this get together is for your friend and this person. There's nothing more, except there's everything and more.

Your friend and her crush begin to talk during the hangout. You are talking to another friend, but your eyes keeps on shifting back to them. Not because you're excited that they are finally talking but because you are a little bit scared. You begin thinking to yourself, "are they actually going to date?" "They look cute together, and she sure is beautiful." And although you would let her love him, you can't help but think that she's opened the door to your right person, your boy.

The next day, she tells you how close they've gotten. You don't tell her that you talk to him too, maybe a little bit too much. You are trying hard to suppress your feelings, you are so desperate for them to leave. In fact, so desperate that you go home and ask God to erase those feelings. When God doesn't, you think it's a sign. However, you're smart enough to know it's not, it's just you remembering how often you've spoken with him. It's you remembering the smile he greets you with, its all the little things, the giggles. But man are you desperate for the feelings to dissipate.

You make the effort to delete your text conversations, but just as you do, a new text appears with his name plastered on your phone screen. You have to tell yourself it's not a sign, it's not God asking you to open the door to your right person.

As weeks go by your friend's feelings intensify, so much so that she has become a reflection of you. She is just in awe of this boy, maybe a little bit too much. It is getting exhausting to pretend this much. Every time she mentions something about him that you already know, you try hard not to laugh or smile and say that you already know.

She tells you, "his favorite movie is Stand by Me" but you stood by him, so you already know. You think about how you guys were racing on the freeway just the other night. It was midnight, there was no one else on the road, just the two of you. He was letting you win, you assume, because your car is older.

The scariest part about that night wasn't getting caught by a police officer; it was getting caught by your friend. You imagined how hurt she would be to see you bond in this way, even though it felt like he was your person. Guilt and infatuation consumed your heart.

When she continues to talk about him, you are thinking that maybe you'll tell her. You don't. Instead, you go home and write a song about him, and hope to God the feelings go away. They don't, only the opposite occurs. She reminds you to invite him to her birthday party. You text him and talk about everything but her birthday party.

The party finally arrives. Everyone is there, looking pretty and privileged, as if the only tragedy that could ever occur is a boy who might not like you back.

He shows up late, and when you see him, you see your friend smiling, happy, the only birthday present she dare wished for. You think to yourself, "let the acting begin" I'm talking Oscars here, and it works for a little bit.

You need to cool down.

You go outside.

You hope no one follows you.

You hope he doesn't follow you.

You hope that maybe he does.

He follows you.

You are angry.

Scared.

Infatuated.

And excited.

When you turn, you see your friend stare at you both through her living room window.

How To Let Go Of Her Boy

I arrived late to the party.

I would be lying if I said I wasn't looking forward to knowing what you looked like now. I heard rumors that you changed, that you had a haircut, and that it made you look a bit more chiseled. I heard that you were a little taller, got a new job, purchased a new car and matured plenty.

It's not like I went around asking every mutual friend how you were doing. I wasn't sitting around scrolling through my social media feed to see if you uploaded a new picture of you or possibly someone else.

I just knew you were invited to this party and so was I, and I would be lying if I said I wasn't looking forward to knowing what you looked like now.

I heard you were doing well, that you were growing up. I knew you would. I prayed for you, and my prayers reached God better than your hands ever reached for mine.

All of our friends were at this party. The Vegas sun had just settled down, and all we were left with was a sandy, yellow afternoon that made our skin look like we had just bathed in gold. We all looked so beautiful. I wouldn't have thought I'd grow up to be the girl with all the handsome boys and girls as friends, but here we were hugging and laughing.

Man, did we look pretty and privileged. I remember that backyard like it was yesterday: the alcohol, the fire pit, the bistro lights, summer vacation and the you and me.

When you walked in, no type of infatuation had held hostage to my eyes. I wore my favorite dress, but your jaw didn't drop, and my heart didn't stop. You were just a boy, a regular boy. And I was just a girl, a regular girl, at least your eyes would argue so.

And so here we were. I can't believe I had spent a whole summer hoping you would fall in love with me, trip on your shoelaces for me, climb on top of our college building and almost die professing your love for me. I can't believe I wanted it so. I can't believe I almost risked a friendship for a boy who didn't know how to say I love you back, even though he said it first. I can't believe I believed in it so.

But here we were, laughing, no longer stealing glances at each other, no longer wondering if we would find time to sneak past our friends and look into each other's eyes, no longer worried if my lips were too dry or if I should wipe what I already had on. No more anticipation, no more sneaking into the bathroom to fix my hair. No more lying to our friends about this; whatever "this" was had finally come to pass. As we danced the night away, I pictured you falling in love with someone that wasn't me, and it didn't hurt. Mostly because I pictured myself falling in love with someone that wasn't you, and it didn't hurt. Finally, I could see the whole picture. Finally, I understood it would have never worked out. Finally, I understood that I was infatuated with this boy, it certainly wasn't love.

It was finally understanding that I will be on time to open the door for my right person. It was finally understanding that my friend could never open the door to my right person. I drove back home that night, happy to have experienced it all. Happy to have written a beautiful song about a boy I once thought was gorgeous, crooked smile, pimples and all. Laughing at myself for wanting it so, but also proud of myself for admitting it so.

Oh how silly; I was in love with an idea and not a boy. He could finally be hers if he was still for the wanting, because I had finally let go of her boy.

The Day My Mother Died

It happened; kind of the same way I've seen it happen in movies. We all stood in the private waiting room. I knew I had lost her from the moment I saw her on life support. Her eyes bulged out of her face, however, I still tricked my brain into thinking that she would get off life support. As I sat there, angry with God and myself, I tried to think of all the positive stories I read about people who made it through life support.

It was the first time in my life that I shit my pants. No one tells you that it's an actual thing, I was so nervous that I ran to the bathroom and literally pooped. I was furious with myself and in disbelief that in the middle of my mother being on life support; my moronic body found it necessary to take a huge dump.

And mind you, before being stuck in the hospital with much anguish, I had been constipated for two weeks and hadn't eaten in three days. I know I shouldn't write much about poop, because it's uncomfortable, but it's safe to say that I find it more pleasant than writing about my mother's death. When she passed, my big sister walked up to us stronger than I ever imagined her to be and said, "Guys, it's time to say bye to Mama."

I remember I couldn't walk, my hand reached for the air in hopes of grabbing my mother's celestial body, but there was nothing. I reached out for God's hand to walk with me into that ICU room, but his hands weren't there, and so my body crippled itself into a form so foreign you'd think I was on the set of "The Exorcism."

My body moved like it had been possessed by someone who had never walked before. Finally, this external body found my mother's external body. She looked... gone. The person I knew, the person I highly respected and loved so deeply left. In front of me laid a body that looked like a puppet, and it was icy and hard; I know because I touched her hand in hopes she'd wake up. She didn't.

The next thing I remember was the nurse dragging me on the floor, and another ICU nurse quickly pulling up a chair for me. I sat there making a fool out of myself as if I've never seen someone die before, that's because I've never seen someone die before. Let alone a woman I have been so in love with. Oh, I was furious; I wailed in that ICU room, played trampoline on that cemented floor.

I dropped, I rolled, I unintentionally kissed the floor. Death is hard. You figure it would be, but you don't realize how hard it is until it happens to you. I never knew my heart could beat that fast and I'd still survive. I never knew my body had an earthquake inside of it. It shook my bottom cheeks, my cheeks, and all the chubs I never knew I had.

Finally, my body was tired. My family and I went back to the waiting room, and it was silent. We all knew there was nothing we could say to each other that would help our broken hearts. How is it that my mother loved us so well that we were all so silently broken? Why did she do this to us? Did she not know that it would cause our hearts to bleed into the sunrise the day she would pass?

I stood by the glass window, and by six-thirty in the morning, the sun rose; it felt like a slap in the face. The same way I knew I could never touch the sun, I would now never be able to touch my mother. I wouldn't be able to laugh with her, watch Judge Judy with her, stay up past twelve and talk to her.

I stood there and thought to myself, "who do I call first?" How embarrassing that it had to end like this. How unfair. Why has this pain been embedded in me? To whom did I have to sacrifice this virgin blood? Who had I harmed to an extent to feel like I've swallowed a knife, and now it is stuck to my gushing throat even my spine can feel it? Who did I have to kneel to? What went wrong, why us? Why my loving mother? Could this have been the pain of knowing God? Did I want to know God after this? Would I have liked to know anyone at all?

It had been a sleepless night for all, all but my mother. My father's eyes had never looked so…gone. Almost like his spirit had wandered off in search of the woman he had known for thirty-six years. It was silent, kind of like the day after a tornado.

No one knew what would occur next. It was sad, what other word can I use? Sorrowful! Depressing! Despair! I sat there witnessing everyone I loved in pain, knowing I had no band-aid for their wound; I hadn't even sanitized mine. I slept maybe for ten minutes, but I wish I had not slept at all.

I woke up to my boyfriend and best friend's text messages, asking for updates and why they hadn't heard from me. Would I be able to kiss my boyfriend again? Go out with my friends past nine? I thought of a million ways my life was about to change. I went outside to catch some polluted air. I sat on the concrete floor and shut my eyes. If I smoked, right now would have been a good time to let a cigarette part my lips. If I were a drug addict, I'd inhale, snort, pump, and swallow whatever I could not to feel anything. However, I'm not any of those things.

I just sat there waiting for God to speak to me, but instead, an ant crawled on my leg. And for the first time, I didn't feel bigger or better than this ant. We were the same size. Perhaps this ant might argue with me, but I felt smaller than it. My mother passed on September 20th, 2018. On the 19th, she laid her head on my shoulders and gave me a hug; I just wish I knew it was a goodbye.

The 3rd Grade Teacher

I walk into work a little later than I should. I try to avoid the principal because I don't want her to notice that I've shown up late this entire week. Usually, I'm known to be the teacher that dresses up a bit too much, especially since I'm not really a teacher.

This entire week, I have not tried at all, I've put on whatever is inside of my closet that won't offend the mothers or interest the fathers. As I race to get to my classroom, the 3rd-grade teacher reminds me that my shoes are not appropriate for work, I don't get offended by this. She's the type of person that follows the rules without asking why they are there, and she expects the same from her colleagues and students.

I'm the type of teacher who tells the 3rd graders that I think the rules are stupid too. Not because I'm desperate for their approval, but because school leaders can sometimes forget what it was like being a kid at a school that felt more like a prison.

As I walk the hallway, I see the administrative assistant stare, still confused as to why I was hired. I can tell that my presence bothers her, which bothers me, and in return, causes me to never actually make eye contact with her. I know she thinks I'm complicated. I know among them my timidity can appear as ill-mannered, especially when 12pm hits, and I run to eat lunch inside of my hot car instead of conversing with other teachers in the staff room.

The 3rd-grade teacher will remind me repeatedly that I need to talk to more people than just her. I tell her I'll go eat at the staff lounge if she promises to talk to me. As we sit and eat, I tell her that I am no longer greeting Sofia's mother because she is rude and looks down on me. The 3rd-grade teacher tells me not to take offense because she does it to everyone; the best thing to do is kiss her bum. I quickly disagree.

The following day I don't greet Sophia's mother, a miserable-looking lawyer who wants to make sure she appears threatening to me. She doesn't like this skinny, young, black girl as the teacher's aide. The 3rd-grade teacher believes its my ego, but I've figured that when someone wants to pretend that you aren't there, the best thing to do is not be there. And so if anything, I am helping Sophia's mother.

The 3rd-grade teacher walks with persistence; she loves her job. She has shown me that you don't have to love children to love the work. She loves the work, she does impressive activities, and laminates everything. She's not really into giving children hugs. She never talks about how cute they are, she ignores their cute letters and compliments. All she ever does is follow the rules and hope to God she is praised by admin. I want to tell her that administration doesn't give a shit about her, but more eloquently, of course.

The third grade teacher tells me that she will probably die at this school. I wish I could tell her that they will have no place to bury her here, because while she gives her all, they still treat her half. "You're part of the problem," I tell her. She complains to me but would never address it to those above her.

I cannot believe the corruption I have seen at a place where children play. If only the children knew how many paper cuts these teachers have had, and they can't even pay their mortgage.

I wish these parents knew the disrespect thrown at these teachers go back home with them, along with ungraded papers. I wish they knew that this aide, who isn't really a teacher, has had to pick up all the dirty work and wear many hats. With no praise or raise, just a mother who can't even greet me because she's a lawyer, or maybe because her husband can't stop staring. Who knows. But if only she knew that same day she decided to ignore me, her daughter had a massive nose bleed at a playground so dirty I'm surprised she still pays tuition. If only she knew the girl she doesn't greet was responsible for cleaning up that bloody mess while trying to keep twenty-five other children away from that area.

If only she knew that this aide had to revisit her daughter's math packet and work with her one-on-one because the licensed teacher had lost her patience. If only she knew I exhausted myself trying to help her daughter with math. If only she knew how much I hated math, only then would she understand that none of this was being done for the luxury.

That same month, I wanted to quit but told myself to stay; they ended up firing me anyway. I remember the administrative assistant's face light with satisfaction. The 3rd-grade teacher came up to me frustrated at how they could do this to her, how she needed the help, that they would most likely make her finish the school year by herself now that I was gone.

She complained about how they always look out for themselves, how she has worked there for twenty years and has only taken five days off for sick leave. "They won't bury you here," I tell her as walk away to rush to my car and cry.

"You are the nicest thing I could ever do for myself."

-Peter McWilliams

Crushes On Buses

The first boy I ever liked also liked me back, but he told me in secret. On the school bus, he didn't save a seat for me; instead, he laughed along with everyone else when I had no place to sit. He looked at me like a world he could see from afar but no matter the miles he ran, he would never actually get there. So he figured he'd just conform to the belief of his peers who believed that this world did not exist because they took no time to acknowledge it.

There's no science here, just a boy who liked a girl that was too weird for him to admit that he liked her. Possibly even loved, because you wouldn't believe the amount of time he'd spend hiding just to sneak my favorite snack in my locker. There's no romance here, just magic. I kind of liked it. I enjoyed being a secret, a mystery that he and I only knew about.

I was never the type of girl who dreamt of kissing pretty boys, but I wanted to kiss that one. There were no flaws to his hair, his smile could conceive a whole new sunset, and when he walked, his feet danced to the rhythm of everyone else's insecurities.

Everyone thought he was beautiful, I thought he was so pretty. I liked how he wore sunglasses in the hallway. No matter how cool and popular he was, there was still a part of him that was a secret, and I'm not talking about me. He applauded me in secret, secrecy was our favorite language. I'd sneak in little notes of love and lyrics, and I'd watch him get on the bus with some of the coolest kids. And when the coolest kids weren't looking, he looked at me. Sometimes I wish he looked at me when the cool kids were looking. I guess I kind of lied; I didn't always like being a secret.

The second boy I ever liked always knew I liked him, possibly even loved because you wouldn't believe the amount of effort I put into looking pretty for social gatherings I did not care for.

I showed up to everything and stared at him like a starving child the first time they see food. I had a big appetite for him. I wanted to tell him that I loved him. I was so infatuated, I forgot that stars existed. I wanted him, and he knew because he always tried to get me alone but mutual friends and homogenous panic attacks made it difficult for us to love.

He became my best friend; the person I spent most of my time with that summer, in secrecy, of course. No one knew that our handshakes turned into high fives, and our high fives into hugs and our hugs never turned into kisses. It's fine anyway, his teeth were crooked, but I liked them that way.

He was selfish, always touched my hair without allowing me to touch his; he never said I love you back, even though he said it first. Never let me hold his hand, even though he held mine first, in secrecy of course.

He wasn't pretty, but his smile reminded me of every song I loved. Truth is, I finally grew up and stopped liking boys who only liked me back when their friends weren't looking. I wanted to be loved in public, the way the girls in the books I read about were loved.

In novels, girls like me got to dance under the stars and kissed in public, not just in front of flowers but next to those picking them too. I finally had to decide who gets to love me and how they get to do it, and the stars staring while the water sprinkler comes on at dusk was no longer enough public for me.

The next boy that loves me will be a man. He will declare his love for me in front of those that say I am unworthy. He won't just save a seat for me on the school bus but a whole row, because he knows this girl has had a lot of backpacks to carry. He will love me misfit and fitted.

Turns out that you don't always want to be the mystery, the "curious at night" girl. The "I could really love this girl if I didn't have the friends that I have" type of girl. Turns out that sometimes you want him to kiss you in public, even if public is just his best friend that talks too much, or his sister, or even God. If he's afraid to admit to God that he loves you, he'll never let you know. So how will you let go of another boy who will run away from a world he could see from afar but no matter the miles he ran, he would never actually get there? Forgetting that to run, you have to use your feet.

The Sweetest Dough

Mom is Dead, but I've bounced back, just like my donut dough. I've risen quite nice. I'm smooth and round, and although I still have a hole in the middle of my dough heart from a heartbreak so hard, I've smiled all week long and have made so many others laugh.

I am as sweet as my dough, and you wouldn't believe how I got here. I got bullied in school, just enough for me to write books. There were boys who liked me, boys who didn't, and a friend who liked me too much I thought she'd either kill herself or me.

I got dragged to parties I did not want to attend, only for me to dance my life away. I became friends with my bullies and became a bully to my friends, and then my friends became my bullies.

My hair fell out, I shaved my head, people stared, and someone fell in love with it. I purchased a guitar and wrote songs for people who didn't deserve it, but I loved my songs and kept them anyway.

I chased Benedicte barefooted in the heat of Laughlin Nevada, which caused me to have blisters. I yelled at her. I wanted to throw a brick wall at her. And in the middle of the night she came to my room, I cuddled with her and prayed the nightmares away, remembering how much I loved her.

I sat in a room full of sick people just to watch my sister smile as her last chemo came to an end. My sister gave birth to a boy so big. I kissed his cheeks, and when I tasted them, they were as sweet as my donut dough.

A man took me to Chicago, and I fell in love with him. We walked in the rain and ate deep dish Pizza. And just like that, I knew I'd be his wife.

My mother died, and indeed it was hard, but this girl rose into the sweetest dough. No, I will not play the victim. The sun is shining on me. My mom used to call herself the Five-Star Lady, and the nights I can't sleep she tucks a star under my pillow.

I'm so grown. I no longer believe in the tooth fairy, but I know the star fairy is real because she gave birth to me. And I'm a star! Just like the cookie-cutter pressed into my donut dough.

A little bit of sugar made me sweeter. That little bit of yeast woke me up and that stick of butter made me richer. That cracked egg made me fluff with hope, and of course I had to add a pinch of salt because my sweetness can bite. I ended with adding flour and water to remind myself that this dough can stretch, no matter what it's gone through. The only brown sugar you'll find in this dough is me. I'll be sweet to you, always available to give you a hand, and although I don't have a band, I'll always cheer for you and your hope.

With all the backpacks I've had to carry, there's no point in being sour. I'll be nice to you. I'll be the sweetest dough you've ever tasted, so have a donut with Diane!

Peaches

I am not sure how this man managed to get me here, but I'm here. I'm not sure where here is, but I'm elsewhere, laughing, and I want to kiss this man. If his hand isn't the strongest I've held, I'll hold no other. Give me this one.

So this is what safety feels like. I always thought home were dusty novels, Vegas traffic, and too much fruit snacks for my mouth. But instead, it's a blue-eyed man and a passenger seat inside a white Prius where I can rest my head and fall asleep while he does all the driving.

And I've fallen asleep comfortably. It's the type of sleep where I really hope I don't pass gas, but it's also the kind of love that if I do, he'll kiss me anyway. There's a lot of things I've never tried that I'm trying with this man, like love.

Driving thirty-six hundred miles with someone isn't always easy but this has been. If I'm not allowed to say perfect, I'll say it anyway, any day, especially today. We've bought peaches from an Amish farm in Texas. These are the best peaches I've ever eaten in my entire life. They are almost as sweet as him. I could hardly contain my joy for these... peaches.

There are men forty-four whose hands feel like four, there are men twenty-four whose hands feel like forty, and this man is one of them. I'll let him eat as many peaches as he desires. I want his lips to be forever sweet to me when I kiss them. No apples welcomed here, just ripened peaches. No need to expel ourselves from this garden of Eden if it's the greatest peace we've ever encountered. And it just might be, at this moment, with the juiciest peaches and a man whose eyes are as kind as his hugs.

And I love them, his eyes, I mean.
And I love them, his hugs, I mean.
And I love him.

If his hand isn't the strongest I've held, I'll hold no other. Give me this one.

The sweetest peach I've ever tasted.

I Love
Eating
With
You

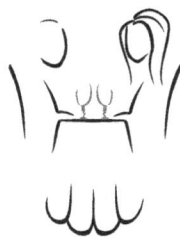

I never knew that food could be so funny, but here we are laughing staring at this delicious Pizza; you can have the first bite and last. I love you.

We compare it to the previous Pizza place we tried last time. I say it was better, but you disagree. It doesn't matter; it's pizza, and you are sitting in front of me looking better than all the pizza in the world! It's cheesy, I know. The pizza, I mean, but so is love, and so is eating pizza with the one you love. But I'll still eat pizza with you, and all the other foods we've tried. The good ones and the disgusting ones.

It's better to be angry at food together than to be angry at food alone, but we've never missed being thankful that we have food at all and so we're never that angry. Even though it has canceled our dates before, due to tummy aches and things associated with tummy aches, but never heartaches. I love you.

We have a local place we go to. The waiter knows us by name and knows our order by heart, which makes the food ten times better than it is. We never eat without laughing. Our mundane work stories become blockbuster films and Oscar buzzes when we share them in front of each other's plates. When my food tastes better than yours, I let you take more than one bite.

When your food tastes better than mine, you offer me your entire plate.

Your love tastes better than all the candy I tried prior to knowing you. And before knowing you, all the candy in the world tasted sweeter than any man's love. Today, as I sit across from you, I think of the memories we've experienced so far and they make fruit snacks seem like they are the bitterest of sweets I've tasted all year. I love you. From awkward dinner dates to Hell's Kitchen cooking competitions at your house, should I indeed admit that your food tasted better than mine that one night?

In your father's kitchen, we compared which one of us cut the homemade fries better. In your mother's kitchen, you cooked for us a recipe you stole from me. In your grandparent's kitchen, we ate the best breakfast in the world, and in my mother's kitchen you shaped beignet better than me. I'll admit that. And my mom would be proud.

Tonight, we ate more meat than we should have, and we were tired. Dinner consisted more of yawns and red eyes than they did conversation. We sat scanning the room in confusion of this busy and overrated restaurant. Still, it was just another eating experience with you. Sharing an overpriced crème brulee the night before we both have to work in the morning tasted better than the crème brulee itself. Because we had to eat, and we had to eat together. Because I love eating with you.

Mon Amour, Mon Amour

Mon Amour, Mon amour
aujourd'hui je te trouve plus beau

continue à poser ta main sur ma genou
mon cœur bat

les papillons
rire de moi

ils disent que je suis tombé pour toi
et alors
pourquoi ça les dérange
en fait, tout est de leur faute

quand j'ai vu ton visage
ils ont rigolé
c'est peut-être ton amour

Mon Amour,
Mon Amour,

aujourd'hui je vais danser avec toi
regarde les étoiles avec toi
créer des étoiles avec vous
avec toi, je veux tout essayer
avec toi, je veux tout goûter

que ce soit de la glace à la fraise
ou
l'eau de mer la plus salée
avec toi, tout sera doux

Mon amour
Mon amour

Je suis heureuse de t'aimer
Je suis heureux d'être aimé par toi

My Love, My Love

My love, my love.
Today I find you most handsome.

Continue to place your hand on my knee.
My heart beats.

The butterflies laugh at me.
They say that I have fallen for you.

So what, why does it bother them?
In fact, it is all their fault.

When I saw your face,
they whispered
"that could be your love."

My love, my love.
Today I would like to dance with you.

Stare at the stars with you.
Create stars with you.

With you, I will try everything.
With you, I will taste everything,
whether it be strawberry ice cream
or the salty sea.

With you, everything will be soft.
My love.
My love.
I am happy to love you.
I am happy to be loved by you.

HANDS MAN

The first time he kissed me, I squeezed his hands so tight I'm sure I stopped his blood circulation.

I wanted him so bad not to know that I was afraid of his touch.

His hands wrapped around what seemed like my baby fingers. I had only held hands with a boy before.

I held my breath as we kissed; I couldn't hear a thing. The world stopped. My memory at that moment vanished. My skin was pulsing. My blood was rushing. I felt so hot I thought we drowned in lava, but perhaps it was just the first time I had ever felt nirvana.

As my fingernails pressed his arm, I was convinced I added one more scar to his body, but he didn't flinch. He must have understood that he had just kissed a girl whose lips were foreign to a man's tongue.

As our friendship blossomed, his hands explored all the hidden parts of me, parts I didn't want to touch.

Parts I did not dare touch.
Parts I was told not to let anyone touch.

Parts I did not know could be touched until he touched them first.

Touch.
Touch.

Touched, by a man's hand. Handy in all parts I did not know were apart.

My body, unaware and scared. Excited and overwhelmed, yet welcoming each finger one by one.

Head to toe and toe to hip.
Hip to lips and lips to gripped, by a man's hand.

The Wedding Day

It's here, the wedding day. I am sitting in a hotel room
with some of my best girls staring at a grand window,
two hours before I say I do to you.
I do.

Finally, I was on time.
Me!
Me!
Me!
I opened the door to my right person. As it turns out, I
would have always been on time to meet you. If only I
had known when it's the right person you're the only one
who can unlock the door, I wouldn't have been so
worried about another girl opening the door to my right
person.

It's not like I knew you existed, but you?
You are romantic.
As romantic as romance can possibly get.
If I were a cat and had nine lives, I'd like to know you in
all nine of them.
And be your wife.
If not your wife, then at least a friend.
If not a friend, at minimum an affair.
But I am not a cat. I've only got one life to live, and in it
I'm your wife.
And you're the best romance that's ever happened to me.

I've waited for a long time to wear a white dress,
wondering what it would look like; wondering what you

would look like. You don't look like I thought you would.
And that's a good thing.
Me? I am shy and anxious, and some might say cute.
But I am wearing a white dress and I feel beautiful, sexy even.

I am sitting in a hotel room with some of my best girls staring at a grand window, two hours before I say I do to you.
I do.

I waited, what took you so long? Oh, never mind, I'm just glad that you are finally here.
The day is finally here.
I get to be with you.
Finally,
I get to be with myself.
You've kissed me, and I've kissed myself.

I get to dance with you.
Be in love with you.
Walk towards the sun with you.
You've turned me into a romantic.
What have you done?
Don't you know I will now wake you up in the middle of the night to kiss you, tickle you even?
What have you done?
Don't you know I will now write love songs about you, sing them to you even.

I never had to hope that you would trip on your shoelaces for me.
You just always did.
I love you.
Finally.
It's our wedding day. I get to be with you.
Me!
Me!
Me!

ACKNOWLEDGMENTS

I want to thank my husband Ian Gough, thank you for being my best friend and best lover. Thank you for being the man who kissed me when all his friends were looking, but most importantly, thank you for introducing me to peaches. I love you.

I want to thank my siblings who have seen the best and worst parts of me and have chosen both. Without you, the world wouldn't exist. I love you Lady, Prisca, Jaime, Vinny and Petite Ben.

I want to thank Benedicte, you have been the first person to read all my words, the errors and the terrors. My words belong to you.

I want to thank some of my best friends, Clarissa, Natasha, John, Dominic, Shameka, and Alula. Thank you for the endless conversations about God and life.

I want to thank my Nephews and my niece, not only have I been loved by you all, but you have taught me how to love all.

I want to thank all the thousands of kids I've worked with, from preschools to elementary schools. You have taught me patience and peace. Your hugs and high fives are more precious than diamonds.

I want to thank the countless women that have been a part of my life. The moments spent together and conversations that have been shared.

My Papa, thank you for keeping your head high and your heart full, even in moments when it feels empty. Thank you for teaching us how to be kind. You are so nice. Sweet even.

My Mama, my star. Thank you for loving me so well. Thank you for teaching me how to live life. It hurt so bad when you left us. I will always love you. Thank you for making me a star.

Last but not least, thank you God. Even in moments of impurity and disgust, your love reminds me that I am yours always.

ABOUT THE AUTHOR

Diane Kiaku Gough is a LasVegas based author. She was born in Africa and raised in Las Vegas. She is a happily married newlywed and is one of six kids. Besides writing, she spends her spare time recording a podcast called "Donuts With Diane" which can be found anywhere where podcasts are available. She enjoys baking, learning how to roller skate, playing her guitar and spending time with family and friends. For inquires please contact Dianekiakubooks@gmail.com

www.ingramcontent.com/pod-product-compliance
Lightning Source LLC
Chambersburg PA
CBHW030106070426
42448CB00037B/1165